TM & copyright © by Dr. Seuss Enterprises, L.P. 2020

All rights reserved.
Published in the United States by Random House Children's Books,
a division of Penguin Random House LLC, New York.
The artwork that appears herein was first published in various books by Dr. Seuss.

Random House and the colophon are registered trademarks of Penguin Random House LLC.

Visit us on the Web!
Seussville.com
rhcbooks.com

Educators and librarians, for a variety of teaching tools, visit us at
RHTeachersLibrarians.com

ISBN 978-0-593-12328-7

MANUFACTURED IN CHINA   10 9 8 7 6 5 4 3 2   First Edition

# Dr. Seuss's

# Every Voice

# COUNTS!

## Make Yourself Heard!

Random House New York

Every voice counts.
You can **TALK** . . .

or **SING** . . .

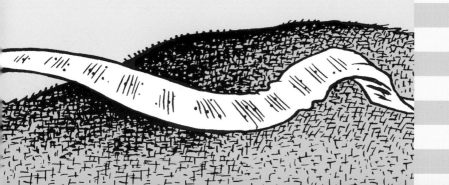

or **SHOUT**.
Loud or soft,
your voice counts.

# You are unique.
# Your voice is UNIQUE.

# And when you join your voice with others, **BIG** things can happen.

Use your voice
to make **CHANGE**.

**SPEAK UP**
for those who
can't speak
for themselves.

Be a **TEACHER**.

Be a
LEADER.

# Use your voice
## to **SHARE** ideas . . .

# and your ears
# to **LISTEN** to others.

# Maybe you'll **LEARN** something new.

So open your mouth—
AND your ears!
Because **every**
**voice counts!**